This Was Love

Poems on love, loss and everything in between

Sujona Chatterjee

BookLeaf Publishing

India | USA | UK

Dedication

To my mother, who always encouraged me to fall in love with my unconventional self.

Preface

"This Was Love" is a collection of poems that tenderly explores the many shades of love—the euphoria of falling, the ache of heartbreak and the quiet strength in vulnerability. These verses hold space for your rawest feelings, offering a gentle reminder that you're not alone. Somewhere, someone has loved like you, hurt like you, healed like you. And in these shared emotions, we find comfort, connection and a little bit of magic.

Acknowledgements

Thank you, Suma Narayan, for seeing the writer in me long before I ever imagined becoming one. Your belief planted a seed that has grown into this very book.

To my family, thank you for encouraging me to write—especially on the days I didn't feel like it. Your gentle nudges became the reason these words found their way onto the page.

To BookLeaf Publishing, thank you for creating a space where emerging writers like me can find the courage to share our stories with the world.

To my readers and cheerleaders, thank you for believing in me and breathing life into my words. I am because of you.

If even one poem spoke to your heart, I'd be truly grateful if you left a review—it means more than you know.

1. I Don't Feel That Pain Anymore

I don't feel that pain anymore,
Not that intense at least.
I am saying this to myself today,
But cry, yet again on Saturday.

I wonder do you miss me anymore,
I tell myself that you do.
Because this way I feel better,
And makes the healing process easier.

Would I ever go back to you?
No way, I won't.
You made your choice quite clear,
And I have standards to uphold.

I know that everything happens for the best,
And in time I will know why.
Even though I question everything I have been through,
As being patient is something I am trying to imbibe.

We all find ourselves when someone leaves,
But they take a piece of ourselves with them.
This leaves a void within us so deep,

That reminds us to never let ourselves feel this way
again.

Tomorrow is another day,
And I'll embrace it like every other day.
Focusing on the goals I put on hold,
As I was busy focusing on your goals instead.

I wish you a happy and successful life,
As holding on to the past is exhausting.
Someday I know everything will make sense.
And you will see me rise from the ashes.

2. Teardrops on My Pillow

After a long day,
When your head lies on the pillow.
You are forced to think of nothing,
And teardrops reach the pillow.

How many nights go by,
And how many days we cry.
The pillow doesn't judge,
Just soaks in all our tears.

Imagine if our emotions had colours,
And the tears would leave a stain.
When we would wake up next morning,
Our pillows would reveal our pain.

Thank goodness that doesn't happen,
And the pillow hides all our secrets and emotions.
It doesn't judge our pain,
Unlike humans who would comment on each mistake.

The pillow knows the nights,
We spend in ruminating our life.
As we toss and turn to get some sleep,
The pillow moulds itself to provide comfort and ease.

The pillow rests our head,
But what it truly does is give us space.
Space to feel our deepest emotions,
That we hide in public spaces and situations.

Teardrops on our pillow,
Are like our journal entries.
They dry the next morning,
And leave us lightheaded and smiling.

Teardrops on my pillow,
Stay anonymous as you are.
Because you're the only space,
Where I can shed all my pretense and reveal all scars.

Goodnight, sleep tight,
While the pillow waits for you.
Hopefully, it soaks in happy tears,
And you heal from your deepest fears.

3. When Nothing Makes Sense in Life

Staring at the blank page,
You question your existence.
You wonder where you are headed,
And feel life is clueless.

You dive into meditation,
Searching for answers you seek,
Reassuring yourself everything will work out,
If you only believe.

Everything is unfolding perfectly,
You keep telling yourself,
However, life always has different plans,
And that reassurance seems to tank.

But its in these tidal waves,
That life draws a map.
We aren't supposed to know the outcome,
But just follow the plan.

In the ups and downs and twists and turns,
New wounds open and old memories return.
You question the pain and learn new lessons,

All the while emerging as a whole new person.

Then you sit back and join the dots,
And magically everything connects.
You begin to understand the how and why,
But only when you sit back and analyse the past.

But like that tidal wave,
Life throws you a tsunami of emotions,
Washing away your old lessons,
And making a gateway for new realisations.

Then you go back and tell yourself,
That you are exactly where you are meant to be,
And everything will work out for the best.
If you only believe.

It seems like you are back to square one,
And nothing seems to work as you thought.
But then you look back and tell yourself,
It worked out then and it will work out ahead as well.

4. Ever So Often

Ever so often,
We need to let go.
Maybe through tears,
Or by deleting old pictures.

Ever so often,
We need to forgive ourselves.
Mistakes don't define us,
But what we do about it matters.

Ever so often,
We always deserve a second chance.
If we missed one,
Maybe it wasn't 'the one'.

Ever so often,
It's okay to take a break.
As gadgets need to recharge.
So do we with a nice meal and a chocolate cake.

Ever so often,
It's okay to let the day win.
No matter how hard we try,
We just cannot expect the end we wish.

Ever so often,
Even the sky cries.
If rains can rejuvenate the earth,
Our tears lighten our hearts and rejuvenate the mind.

Ever so often,
Just let yourself be.
As whatever is meant for you,
Will appear at the right moment, you will see.

5. You Broke My Heart on a Winter Night

You broke my heart on a winter night,
It wasn't the cold that made me tremble in plight.
It was so easy for you when you said it's over,
How would you know the gut-wrenching pain my heart
was taking over.

I went home and lay on the bed that night.
Staring at the ceiling while tears clouded my sight.
Every second felt like one minute and a minute an hour.
Time could be my biggest enemy I didn't know so far.

Food feels bland as I have your taste in my mouth.
Perfumes sting me like bees as I once smelled of it after
we made out.
Pretending to live a normal day as people asked what's
wrong.
How do you explain to them that you feel dead like a
meaningless song?

You don't want to fall in love ever again as this hurts so
bad.
You would trade with time to just go back to feeling
loved as you once had.

You feel miserable as you never wanted to feel this
vulnerable.
You feel like wiping the smile off anyone's face,
As you're dying within.

But life has a strange way of moving on,
Like it doesn't care if you're happy or sad as it's meant
to keep you going, no matter what's going on.
You have to get out of bed and face the day head-on,
As it's rightly said what doesn't kill you makes you
stronger if only you believe that you can move on.

6. What Is Life Without a Few Leaps of Faith

What is life,
Without a few risks.
Said by those who have truly lived.

These risks are synonymous,
To leaps of faith.
It's always the unknown element,
That's wrecks our inner mental state.

Some leaps are good,
They excite us to try something new.
Some leaps are terrifying,
And you feel you will faint.

But no matter the consequence,
There is always a learning.
That whether you lose or gain,
A lesson is always taught in unknown ways.

After that first heartache,
You promised to never love again.
But in the process,
You evolved into a much better person.

That friendship you wanted to last forever,
Broke into pieces when jealousy took over.
You felt you won't ever trust again,
But the truth is you identified what you are,
And what you seek in others.

Loss, gain, love and heartaches,
Are the result of that leap we took.
We trusted the universe and told ourselves,
That it is the only way we will get closer,
To our purpose one day.

Leaps of faith then,
Are inevitable.
They appear in mysterious ways,
When we least expect it.
The choice is ours, whether to jump or walk away.
Whatever the decision,
It will always be what is meant in our fate.

7. When You Begin to Enjoy Your Own Company

There is a time in life,
Where everyone is at a different phase.
Some married, some parents and others working all day.

At that moment you may wonder,
Where do you fit in,
As you're still discovering,
Which road will lead you to the end of the tunnel.

While going through the tunnel,
You feel horrible.
It's dark and lonely and you only hear the sound of
footsteps echoing trouble.

Your mind works in ways where you think your
existence is pointless.
As the people you confided in,
Are set to heal others pain and resolve quarrels.

An empty mind is a devil's workshop,
Where Satan becomes the teacher.
It fills the brain with words that are painful,
Like worthless, unwanted and insecure.

They say you need time to discover yourself,
Before the next chapter begins,
If no one is willing to listen to your story,
Take up activities that heal you from within.

Take a walk with birds,
Sip wine with your speakers.
Study a new course,
Or go for a movie without a companion.

You feel you're going insane,
Because you're talking to yourself.
But remember what Dumbledore told Harry,
Of course its happening inside your head,
But why shouldn't it be real?

The point I am trying to make is,
This phase will teach you how to love yourself.
As when you begin enjoying your own company,
You discover an undiscovered form of independence.

8. My Heart Is Tucked Under Your Pillow

Let's end it then,
Okay fine you said.
It felt like you were waiting for me to say it,
So that you wouldn't have to instead.

It still baffles me,
That it was so easy for you to leave.
But you left me in pieces,
That I had to pick up to heal.

Each piece has your imprint on it,
One has your lingering smell.
Of your perfume mixed with sweat on your shirt,
That you left with me when we last hugged.

Do you remember,
The sunrise and sunsets we shared on your bed?
When I kissed you goodbye,
I left my heart tucked under your pillow.

It felt like you never left,
You used to say this the next time we met.
I still need to collect that piece under your pillow,

But then I realised it will always be there.

I cannot unlove you I realised it over time,
As my love for your will never die.
I will always wish well for you,
Even though our paths will never collide.

My love is intense you knew it from the start,
Which is why you would say,
I have never met anyone like you who loves this hard.
Maybe that's why you felt we must end this, quick,
As receiving so much love was too much for you to
handle.

9. Where Do You Keep Your Shame?

Where do you keep your shame?
Wait, let me tell you where I keep it.
So that you will feel at ease,
When you reveal it.

I hide it in my phone's notes as journal entries,
Where no one can look or judge.
Its my feelings and interpretation,
Of the situations life threw at me all at once.

A forbidden kiss,
Was it a mistake?
Or was it an outlet of pain?
A rude conversation,
A confession session,
Where I expressed my feelings without shame.

I knew what I give out,
Will also give me,
Reactions of surprise and hate.
Some people left,
But their memories didn't leave me,
So, I write down all my pain.

But why should we feel ashamed of those mistakes?
They made us who we are.
We now know what we mustn't do,
Would we have learnt if we never crossed the bar?

Do you feel shame?
Let's talk about it,
Then my guilt will start to diminish.
Then I will know that feeling shameful is normal,
And there is no need to feel shame about our shameless
actions.

I went first,
And told you my secret,
Its time we learnt a bit about yours.
Remember, you weren't right or wrong,
The situation was such that you reacted,
In a manner that made you feel strong.

We all stumble, all feel broken,
And none of us have it all figured out.
Let's talk about it, let's heal from it,
As when we share, we teach and learn,
That shame is an integral part of growth,
We cannot walk away from.

10. Honesty Is the Best Policy

Honesty is the best policy,
A phrase that should be used with scarcity.
Think about it and you'll notice,
How being honest has put you in deep atrocity.

If you say the truth,
You're judged.
If you lie, you're honoured.
You tried explaining your side of the story,
But instead, your truth was unheard and buried under
the earth.

Being honest about whom we like or dislike,
Or just saying to a person 'I envy your achievement'.
A simple statement like that could be misunderstood,
And you could land in trouble.

You go home and wonder 'I was just being honest'.
You learn that this trait will ruin you into pieces.
Don't speak about that book or movie you see.
As a character assassination is just waiting to happen.

But I beg you that if you feel you're capable of such

honesty,
And have fought so hard to maintain that purity.
I know you've lost more rather than hoped to gain,
Hang in there as the rewards will greet you
in unexpected ways.

It's all about timing and you come across someone like
you.
Then you'll understand and say, 'thank god I didn't give
up on my honest attitude'.
As that's how you meet like-minded souls,
Otherwise, you would be drowning in lies surrounded by
ten people and still feel all alone.

11. I Locked My Past Away Inside the Chest

People left,
Heart was broken,
And rejections left a scar.
It's all in the past,
Locked in my chest.
What remains are the lessons,
I learnt so far.

One, everything happens for a reason.
Two, people are like seasons.
Each enter when the time is right,
And leave when the next season arrives.
Through it all life teaches you lessons,
You are born alone, and pain makes you more
independent.
But holding on to the past did no one any good,
Because you then miss out on new experiences,
And the train of life leaves the station.

The past we cannot forget,
And we must not as its now a survival gadget.
It's got an arsenal of experience,
That we need when tough times make an appearance.

Therefore, let's lock the past,
And seal the memories as cases closed.
But let's imbibe the learnings,
And move towards life's next destination.

12. Life's a Journey

Life's a journey,
With no destination.
All one can do,
Is follow its directions.

Then along the way,
It throws us unforeseen curveballs.
Some hit straight to the head,
While the rest pierces the heart.

Then moving forward,
We meet people and situations.
Each teaching us a lesson,
Vital for our growth and survival.

But as we move forward,
Healing happens too.
There is no timeline for the same,
But the intensity of pain reduces day by day.

Today I am here,
Tomorrow I'll be there.
But what remains,
Are the memories we create.

Through the pain, healing,
Crying and venting,
We rise from the ashes.
And then take flight,
Towards life's suggested direction.

13. Why I am Grateful to Those Who Left

People come, people go,
And while that happens,
Our heart becomes sore.

But through it all,
We find the will to survive.
And eventually, the lessons come alive.

Some taught us we are enough,
Some taught us they were never meant for us.

Some taught us we deserve better,
Some taught us we are capable of much more.

All of this wouldn't have happened,
If people didn't say goodbye at the right moment.
We cried and evolved into a person we never thought we
could,
And explored new dreams that opened doors to new
experiences.

Therefore, I am grateful,
To all those who left.

I now realise my worth,
And how much love I must share.
As too much of anything is detrimental to our health,
And it is not selfish if I think about the love, I must give
myself.

14. And That's Why She Chose to Shut-in Her Emotions

There was a girl,
Who believed in true love.
Though her idea of love,
Was based on the books she read,
She smiled when she dreamt,
About her love coming to life.

She didn't know how intoxicating it would be,
How could she when no one held her for so long.
Until she met the man of her dreams,
Who showed her stars in the hot Mumbai sun.

She craved to feel her wild emotions,
And wanted to bottle the smell of passion.
She finally understood what those authors meant,
When they termed love cannot be explained,
But must be felt.

She knew all this was too good to be true,
Her heart shattered when love turned into emotional
abuse.

False promises hurt and words lost their meaning.
And then she understood what authors meant about that
numbing feeling.

While she broke free of the suffocation,
She couldn't forget the raging feelings of passion.
How could she, as now she knows how it feels.
She wondered, it would have been better if she never
knew,
What love does to the heart and how the body craves to
be loved.

She couldn't think nor focus as her mind kept visiting
the past.
Then she decided she must freeze her heart.
As much as she craved to be in love,
It hurt too much, and she decided to shut it all.

Then she refused to feel anything.
When a familiar scent passed by,
She chose to delete all the memories.
She shut herself and created her new world,
Where all that existed was work and new milestones.

People questioned,
But she refused them answers.
When her lover contacted her again,

She couldn't remember what it all felt.

Society termed her cruel and ruthless.

If only they knew how love wrecked her from within.

15. Your Last Call Was Where the Healing Started

I kept staring at my screen,
Hoping to see your name.
Even though I had to get through my day,
I felt my phone was ringing every second.

Then as fate would have it,
I was in a meeting.
I could see the phone ringing,
But couldn't dare to receive it.

As the meeting ended,
I rushed to call you back.
You answered with a deep 'hello',
While I was hiding my tears.

'How are you', you asked,
'I am fine', I replied.
Then a few seconds went by,
And we both knew this is the last call of our lifetime.

'I wish you well', I said,
'I will always love you', you said.
'Then why did you treat me this way', my mind said,

'Goodbye', finally I developed the courage to say.

As the dial tone went blank,
And the waterfall of tears travelled from my eyes to my
neck.
That last call felt like thousand thorns piercing my skin,
And my heart felt like it was choking to death.

Our last call taught me,
That I am resilient and willing to heal.
But healing only happens after the terrible storms,
And your last call was the beginning of it all.

16. Why I Quit Blaming Myself

The fault is yours,
Of course, it is.
I wondered while the fight was going on.
And then I wondered,
Is it ever his fault?
How can someone feel they are right all along?

As the anger fades,
The pain sets in.
As the tears flow,
The heart starts to heal.

And then the veil of self-blame fades,
And the rational mind kicks in.

Stop taking the blame,
You are not wrong.
If my honesty has such a heavy price,
Then the person must be wrong.
If respect flies out the window,
Is there a relationship at all?

I quit,

Those constant self-blame thoughts.
I stood up,
And ended it all.
I realised that when love becomes control,
Walking away is hard,
But it's the vital call.

And then it all appeared,
As the mind and heart had a safe space to feel it all.
Your mind knows when you are wrong,
You know when to apologise,
But you're not to blame for it all.
If the relationship mattered,
The effort would have been both ways.
And the self-blame wouldn't have existed,
As before you could feel the pain,
The fight would have been a distant memory.

17. The Stars in Your Eyes

You were wearing blue.
That was it for me,
To go weak on my knees,
And kiss you goodbye.

But then our order arrived.
And the coffee mug set in front,
Distracted me,
From the stars in your eyes.

I didn't need much.
To know the real you,
After all,
Your eyes said it all.

I knew you loved me.
The moment you hugged me,
Since your warmth,
Travelled from my limbs to my heart.

You set my senses free.
With that perfume,
Filled with musk and citrus feel.
As your hands touched mine,

I wanted to stop time.

I guess now you know,
Why I don't look into your eyes.
I struggle to find words,
And I hate losing when I know I am right.

But if losing means,
Getting lost in your eyes,
I am willing to succumb to defeat.
If you don't question,
Why I didn't choose to fight.

18. Dear You

Dear You,

Tall, black eyes, with a smile to die for,
And yet you hide,
Behind the assumptions of your mind.

When you are lost in that story,
Thinking the world is full of possibilities.
I wish you could see,
The miracles of your journey.

You can inspire,
But still you perspire,
Over opinions and critiques,
That don't see the real you behind your humour.

The way your eyes twinkle,
When you're excited over little things.
The way you uplift others,
With that tone of confidence.
I fall for you all over again,
If only I could show you,
The difference you make.

Don't cry over the past,
The future won't be that hard.
Because you choose to live in the present,
By sharing and learning from the scars.
I wish you would realise,
There is only one you.
That stole my heart,
The moment you said 'hi'.

Yours forever,
The invisible lover

19. The Text That Never Came

You took my number,
And I hoped you would text.
Maybe not immediately,
But before the day ends.

I waited patiently,
Like the tiger waits for its prey.
Only to realise I was the prey,
As my heart was tearing apart.

You may have changed your mind,
Or another woman was the cause.
You may have been in trouble,
Or I was just another option.
You won
But my hope, lost.

It's strange how I still hope,
Your text will arrive.
I pride my heart for its optimism.
Soon this too will die,
Like your memory from my mind.

20. You Leaving Was the Best Lesson of My Life

One text,
Was all it took,
For our hearts to collide.
From good morning,
To good night,
You were the only thought on my mind.

Months passed,
I fell head over heels,
With fear brimming in my heart,
Where all this will lead.

I kept pleading,
For you to never leave.
Your promise,
Was the only comfort,
That put me to sleep.

But as I woke up,
One morning,
Your text tore me apart.
You moved to a new city,
But never asked me, to be a part.

That night I looked up,
The stars never looked so bright.
Its as if they could see my tears,
And decided,
I needed shelter,
In their light.

I blamed them,
And questioned,
About the fault in our stars.
To which they laughed,
And blamed me,
For my oversight.

I should have guessed,
Your love,
Was too good to be true.
As I was blinded by your love,
From night to noon.

Six months went by,
And today,
I looked up again to the stars.
This time they applauded,
For the realisation I had tonight.

You leaving,
Was the only way,
My dreams could take flight.
What I thought was a fault in our stars,
Turned out to be the best lesson of my life.

21. A Night, Where Two Hearts Became One

The day we met,
Not knowing,
Where it all led.
Words all jumbled in the head,
The heart,
Beating million times per second.

But then we uttered a few words,
One, then two and then ten.
Conversations took flight,
Time,
A mere spectator,
And us,
Lost in each other's voice.

We felt magic,
Within.
Our eyes,
Twinkling.
Lost in the warmth of our smiles,
The stars making a special appearance,
To brighten up the night.

Both,
Knew this is meant to be.
And so,
When our phones chimed,
We ignored it with glee.
The full moon,
Casting a shadow of our existence,
And we,
Silently wishing,
This night never ended.

But then,
With a heavy heart,
We did depart.
Although with a promise,
To meet,
When the sun wakes us all.

However,
This night,
Will forever leave a mark.
As Cupid finally won,
In crafting the perfect night.
Where two hearts,
Became one.